Table of Contents

Pineapple Tuna Bites	4
Pineapple Chicken Lettuce Cups	6
Cheddar Cheese Crustless Quiche	8
Hawaiian Breakfast Wrap	10
Almond Date Coffee Cake	12
Pork Chops with Pineapple Salsa	14
Pineapple Apricot Glazed Ham	16
Citrus Barbecue Chicken	18
Polynesian Meatballs	20
Bulgur Wheat with Pineapple, Pecans and Basil	22
Carrot Date Slaw	24
Watergate Salad	26
Easy Upside Down Cake	28
Easy Pineapple Rice Pudding	30

Pineapple Tuna Bites

Prep: 20 min.
Makes 24 appetizers

- 1 can (6 oz.) tuna packed in water, drained and flaked
- 2 tablespoons (1 oz.) cream cheese, softened
- 2 tablespoons mayonnaise
- 1 jar (23.5 oz.) DOLE® Pineapple Chunks
- 2 tablespoons chopped almonds
- 24 small round crackers

- **COMBINE** tuna, cream cheese and mayonnaise in medium bowl, mixing well. Chill, if desired, until ready to serve.

- **MEASURE** 1 cup drained pineapple chunks; stir into tuna mixture with almonds. Spoon mixture onto crackers; serve.

Nutrients per serving:

Calories 190
Total Fat 5g
Cholesterol 10mg

Sodium 450mg
Carbohydrate 27g
Dietary Fiber 1g

Sugars 4g
Protein 9g

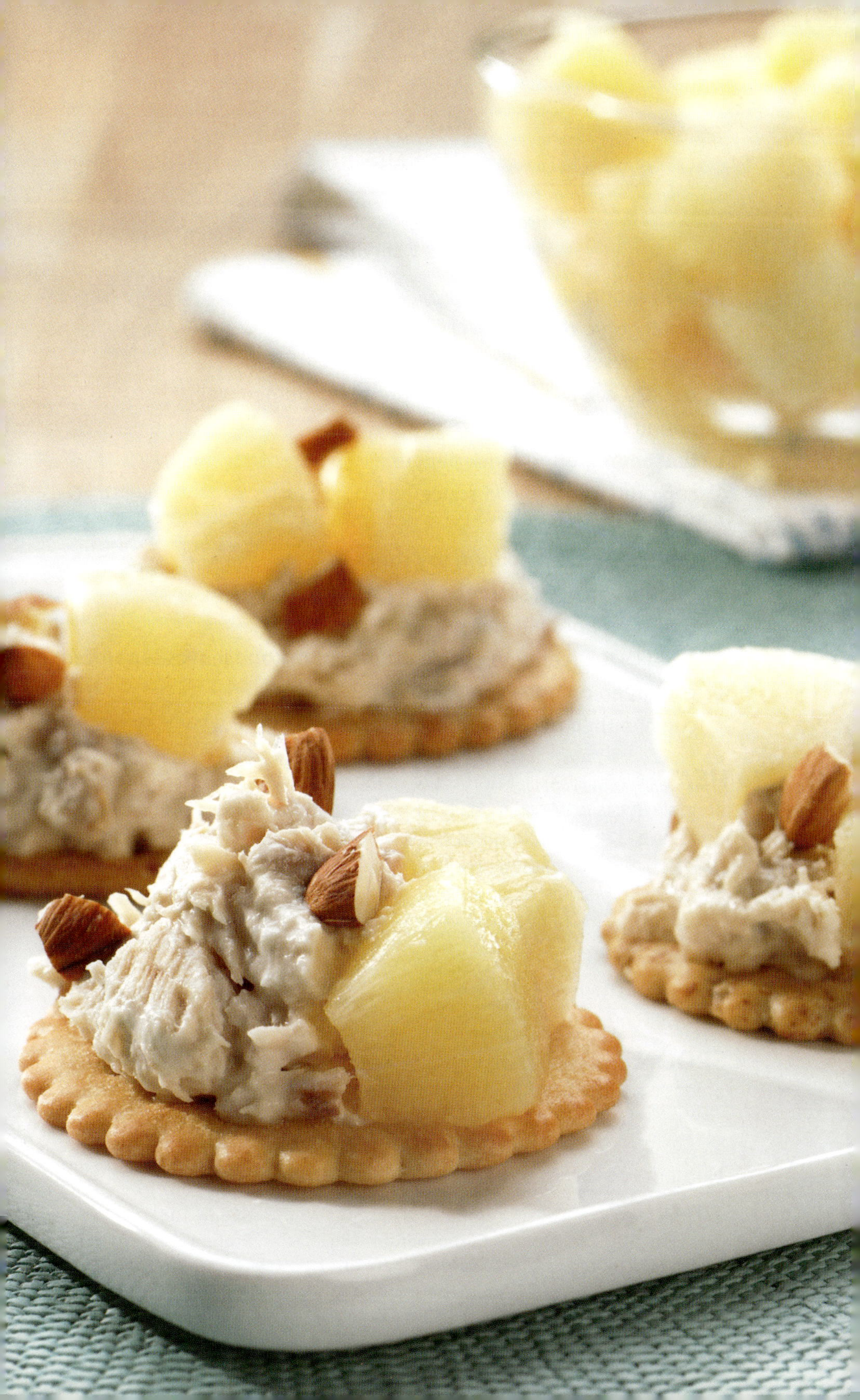

Pineapple Chicken Lettuce Cups

**Prep: 10 min. • Cook: 20 min.
Makes 8 servings**

- 1 tablespoon olive oil
- 4 small garlic cloves, finely chopped
- ½ cup coarsely shredded DOLE® Carrots
- 1 can (20 oz.) DOLE Crushed Pineapple, drained well
- 1 pound ground chicken
- 1 teaspoon ground black pepper
- ½ cup prepared teriyaki sauce
- ¼ cup rice vinegar
- 2 tablespoons low sodium soy sauce
- 1 tablespoon dark sesame oil
- 1 teaspoon hot chili sauce
- 1 head DOLE Iceberg Lettuce, stems cut off and leaves separated
- ¼ cup green onions, finely chopped
- ¼ cup chopped peanuts, toasted (optional)

- **HEAT** oil in large skillet and sauté garlic and carrots for 3 to 5 minutes, or until carrots are tender. Add crushed pineapple and sauté for an additional 3 minutes. Remove carrot mixture to bowl; cook chicken in skillet 10 minutes or until no longer pink and crumbling into small pieces. Season with pepper; drain well.

- **MIX** together teriyaki sauce, vinegar, soy sauce, sesame oil and chili sauce. Stir into ground chicken. Simmer 5 minutes to allow liquid to reduce, and then add carrot and pineapple mixture back to the pan. Stir until well combined.

- **SPOON** chicken mixture into lettuce leaves and garnish with green onions and chopped peanuts. Roll and enjoy.

Nutrients per serving:

Calories 190
Total Fat 10g
Cholesterol 50mg
Sodium 870mg
Carbohydrate 13g
Dietary Fiber 1g
Sugar 10g
Protein 13g

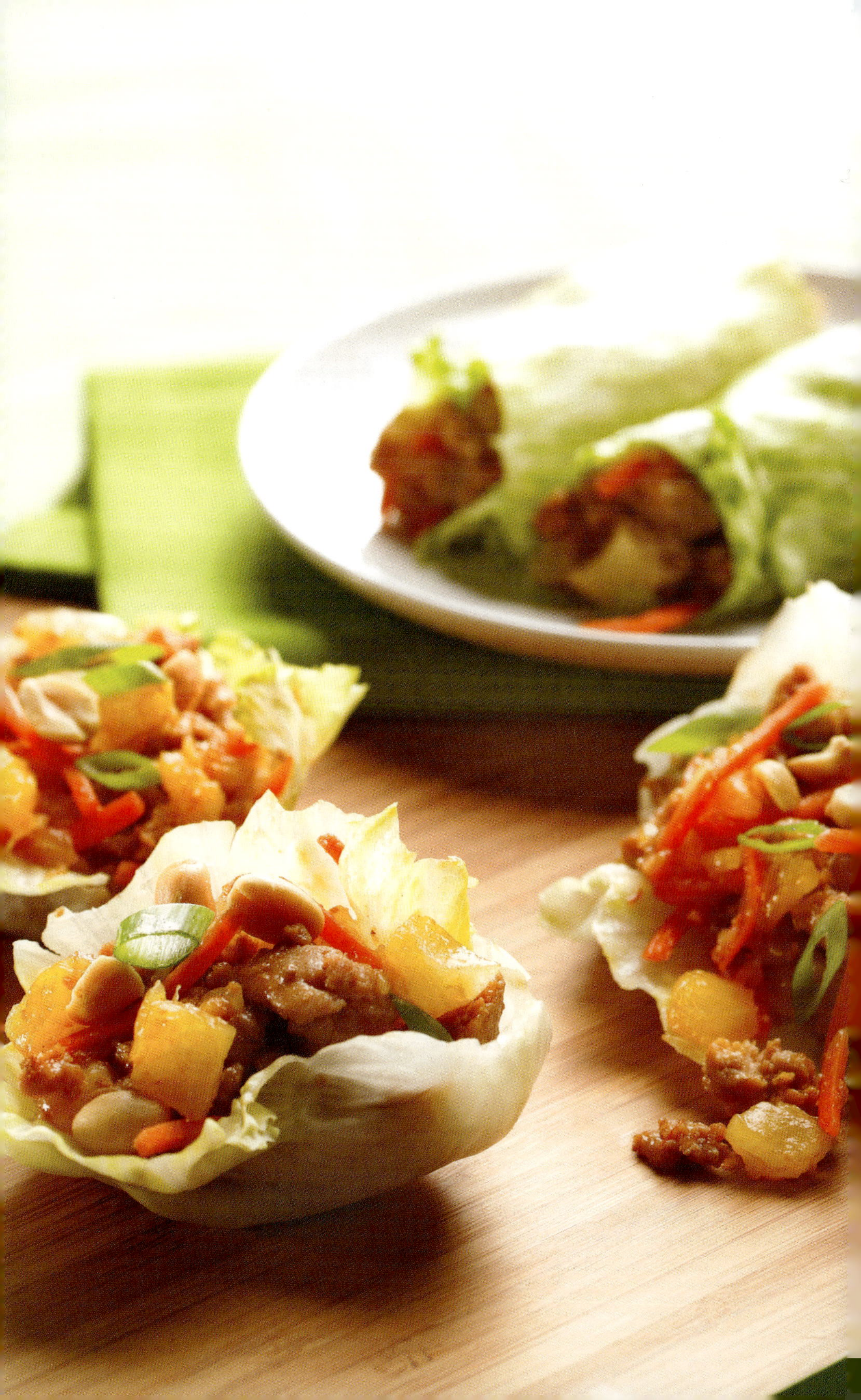

Cheddar Cheese Crustless Quiche

Prep: 10 min. • Bake: 30 min.
Makes 6 servings

- 1 can (20 oz.) DOLE® Crushed Pineapple
- 3 eggs, lightly beaten
- 1 cup sour cream
- ½ cup prepared baking mix
- 3 tablespoons diced green chiles
- ½ teaspoon salt
- 1½ cups shredded Cheddar cheese
- 6 slices bacon, cooked, crumbled
- 2 tablespoons chopped fresh parsley

- **PREHEAT** oven to 400°F. Drain pineapple well, reserve ½ cup pineapple for garnish. Spray 6 individual ramekins or 9-inch baking dish with cooking spray.

- **COMBINE** eggs, sour cream, baking mix, chiles and salt until blended. Stir in remaining pineapple and cheese. Pour into prepared baking dishes. Top with crumbled bacon.

- **BAKE** 30 minutes. Let stand 10 minutes before serving. Sprinkle with parsley. Garnish with reserved pineapple.

Nutrients per serving:

Calories 330
Total Fat 23g
Cholesterol 150mg
Sodium 710mg
Carbohydrate 17g
Dietary Fiber 1g
Sugars 10g
Protein 15g

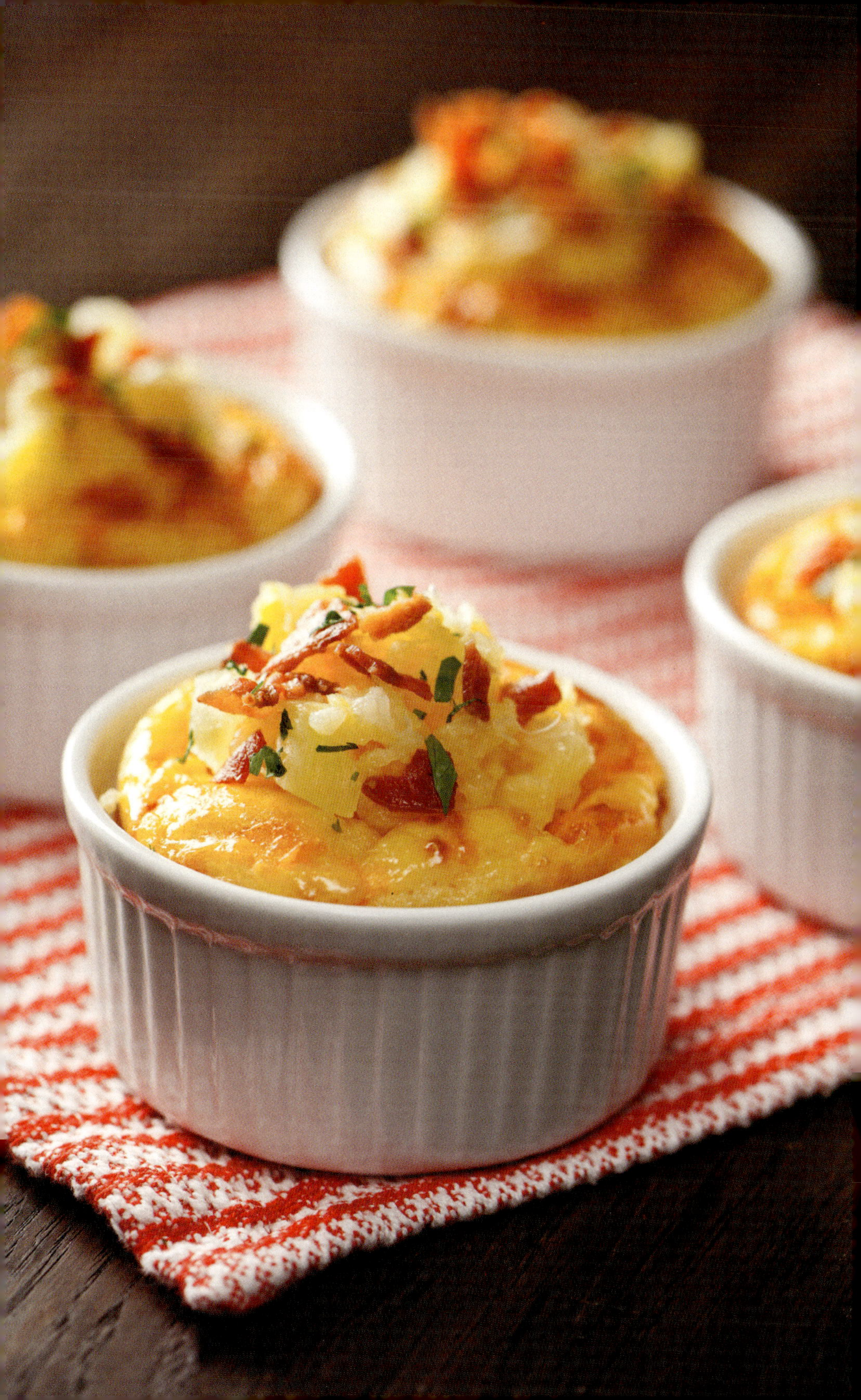

Hawaiian Breakfast Wrap

Prep: 15 min.
Makes 4 servings

- 6 eggs
- ¼ cup milk *or* water
- ¼ cup chopped ham *or* Canadian bacon
- ¼ cup chopped red *or* green bell pepper
- 2 tablespoons butter *or* margarine
- 1 can (8 oz.) DOLE® Crushed Pineapple, drained
- 4 (8-inch) flour tortillas

- **BEAT** together eggs and milk in medium bowl until blended. Set aside.
- **COOK** ham and bell pepper in hot butter in large nonstick skillet over medium heat until ham is lightly browned and pepper is tender-crisp. Stir in egg mixture and crushed pineapple. Scramble until desired doneness, stirring constantly.
- **EVENLY** divide egg mixture onto flour tortillas. Roll sides up. Serve with watermelon wedges and lime slice, if desired.

Nutrients per serving:

Calories 290
Total Fat 15g
Cholesterol 285mg
Sodium 510mg
Carbohydrate 28g
Dietary Fiber 2g
Sugars 7g
Protein 15g

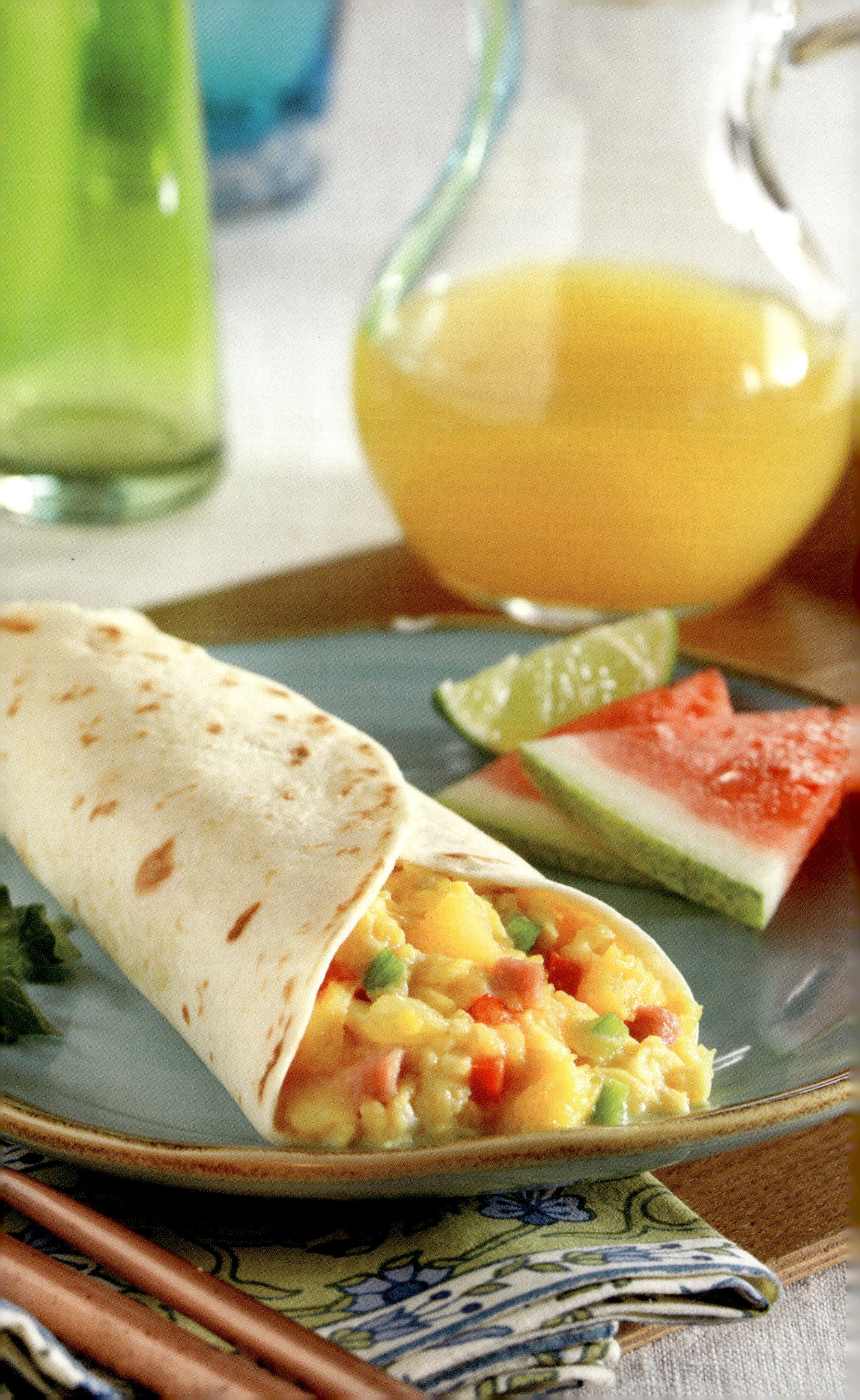

Almond Date Coffee Cake

Prep: 15 min. • Bake: 40 min.
Makes 15 servings

- 1 can (20 oz.) DOLE® Crushed Pineapple
- ½ cup packed brown sugar
- 2¼ cups all-purpose flour, divided
- 1 teaspoon ground cinnamon
- ¾ cup butter *or* margarine, softened, divided
- 1 cup slivered almonds
- 1 pkg. (8 oz.) DOLE Chopped Dates, divided
- ¾ cup granulated sugar
- 3 eggs
- 2 teaspoons baking powder
- ¼ teaspoon ground nutmeg
- ¼ teaspoon salt
- ½ cup low fat sour cream

- **PREHEAT** oven to 350°F. Spray 13×9-inch baking pan with cooking spray.
- **DRAIN** pineapple well, pressing out at least 1 cup juice. Reserve ¼ cup juice.
- **COMBINE** brown sugar, ½ cup flour and cinnamon in small bowl. Cut in ¼ cup butter until coarse. Stir in almonds and half the chopped dates.
- **BEAT** granulated sugar and remaining butter until light and fluffy. Beat in eggs, one at a time, until blended. Combine remaining flour, baking powder, nutmeg and salt. Alternate adding flour mixture, pineapple juice and sour cream to batter until well incorporated. Stir in remaining dates.
- **POUR** cake batter into prepared baking pan. Spoon drained pineapple evenly over cake. Top evenly with almond topping. Bake 35 to 40 minutes, or until toothpick inserted in center comes out clean.

Nutrients per serving:

Calories 340	Sodium 210mg	Sugars 32g
Total Fat 15g	Carbohydrate 50g	Protein 6g
Cholesterol 40mg	Dietary Fiber 3g	

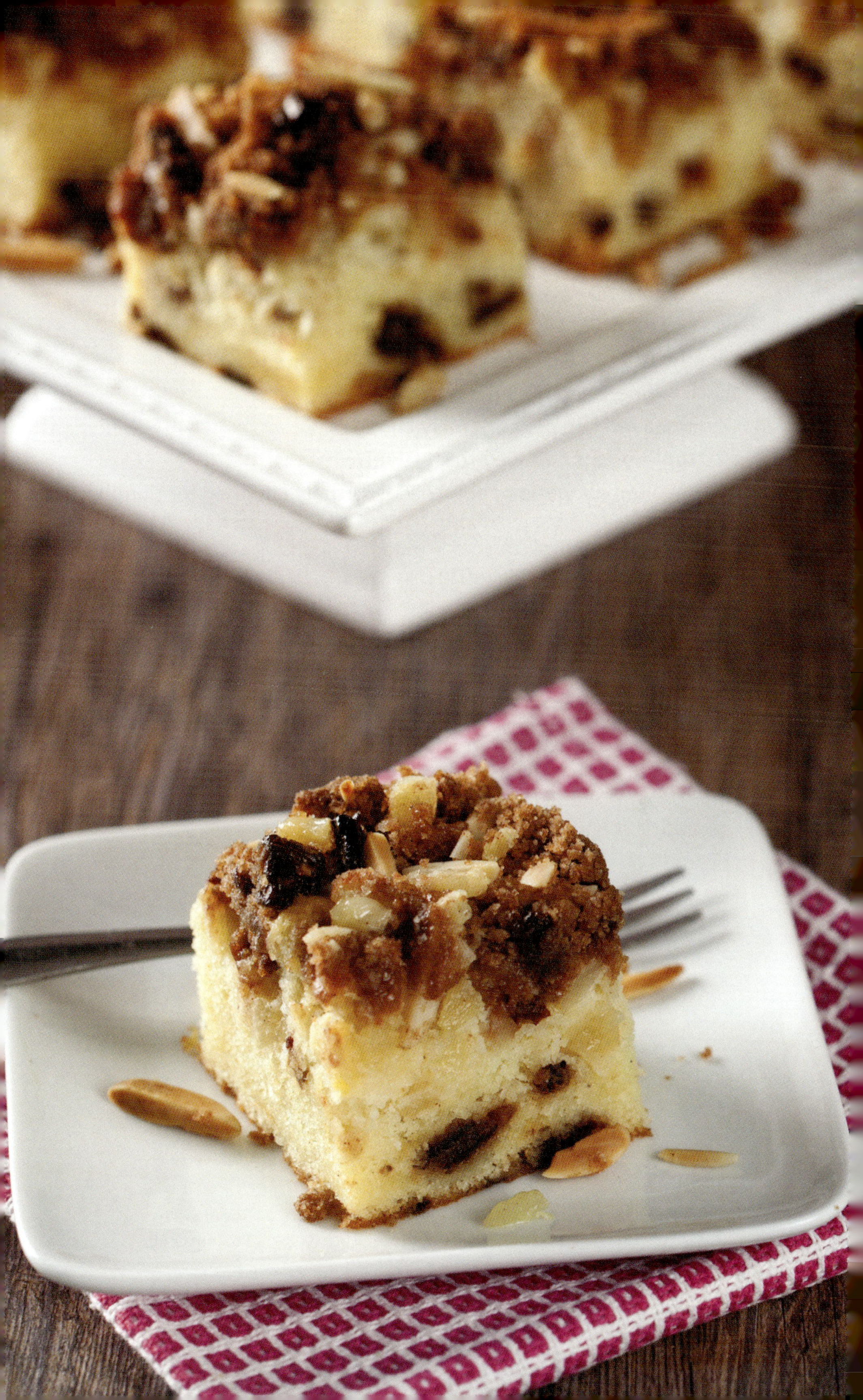

Pork Chops with Pineapple Salsa

Prep: 15 min. • Marinate: 30 min. • Cook: 10 min.
Makes 4 servings

- ¾ cup teriyaki marinade, divided
- 4 boneless pork loin chops, ¾-inch thick
- 1 can (20 oz.) DOLE® Pineapple Chunks, drained, diced
- ⅓ cup finely chopped red onion
- ½ small red bell pepper, finely chopped
- 2 tablespoons chopped fresh cilantro
- 1 medium jalapeño pepper, seeded, finely chopped (optional)

- **POUR** ¼ cup teriyaki marinade over pork chops in a sealable plastic bag. Refrigerate and marinate for 30 minutes.

- **COMBINE** ¼ cup teriyaki marinade with pineapple chunks, red onion, bell pepper, cilantro and jalapeño pepper. Let stand at room temperature up to 1 hour.

- **REMOVE** pork chops from teriyaki marinade, discarding marinade. Grill or broil pork chops 10 to 15 minutes turning and brushing occasionally with remaining ¼ cup teriyaki marinade or until pork reaches internal temperature of 145°F. Discard any remaining marinade. Serve chops with pineapple salsa.

Nutrients per serving:

Calories 233
Total Fat 2g
Cholesterol 51mg
Sodium 1014mg
Carbohydrate 26g
Dietary Fiber 2g
Sugars 22g
Protein 24g

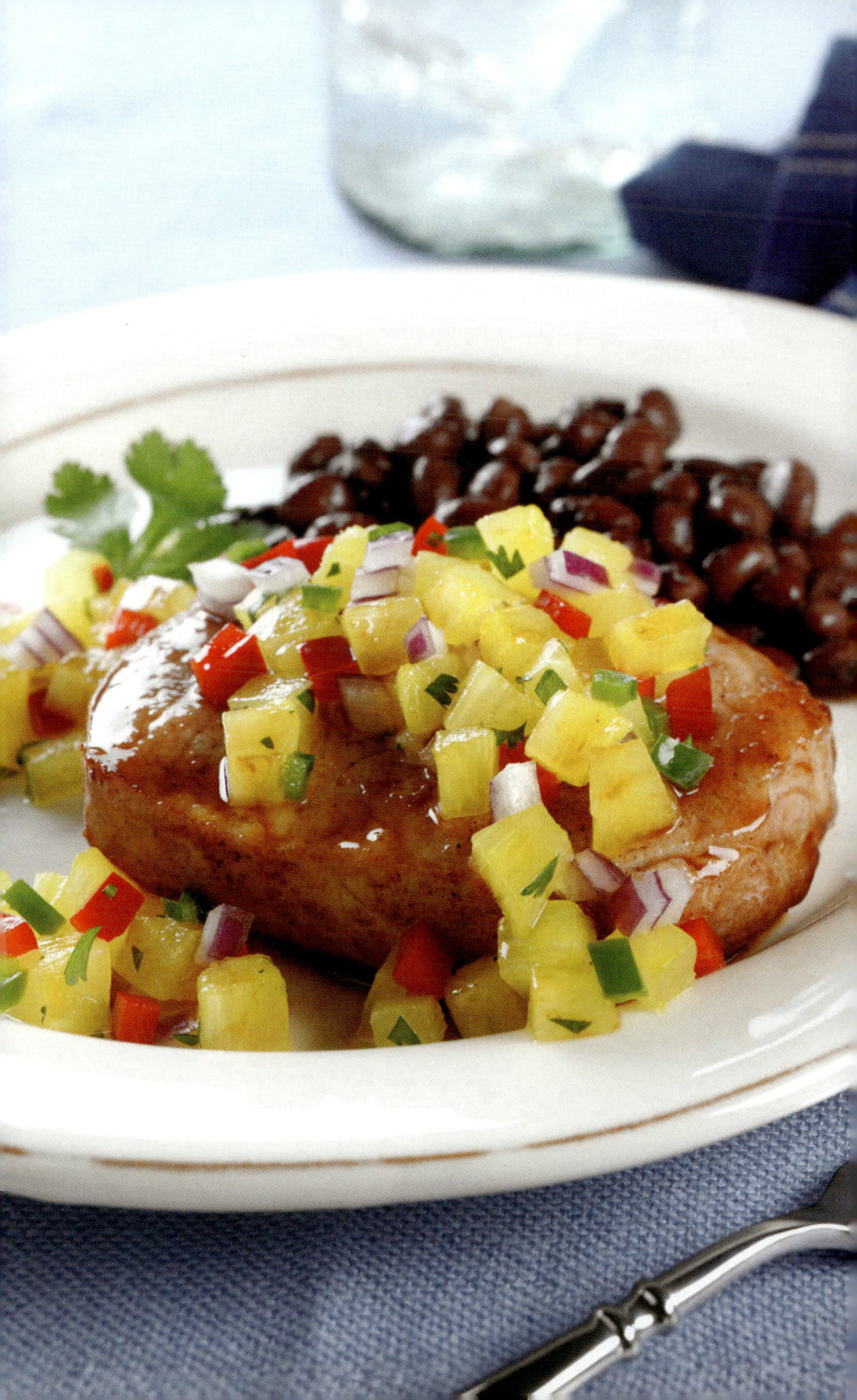

Pineapple Apricot Glazed Ham

Prep: 20 min. • Bake: 1¾ hr.
Makes 16 servings

- 1 can (20 oz.) DOLE® Pineapple Slices
- 1 (5½-pound) ham
- Whole cloves
- 1 cup apricot jam *or* pineapple-apricot jam, divided
- 2 tablespoons balsamic *or* red wine vinegar
- 2 tablespoons honey
- 1 teaspoon cornstarch
- ⅛ teaspoon ground cinnamon

- **DRAIN** pineapple; reserve ¾ cup juice. Chop 4 pineapple slices into small pieces; set aside.
- **SCORE** top of ham in diamond pattern, making ¼-inch deep cuts. Insert cloves into each diamond. Place in shallow baking pan. Brush with ¼ cup jam; cover with foil.
- **BAKE** ham according to package directions. Arrange 6 pineapple slices on top of ham during the last 30 minutes of baking. Brush pineapple and ham with another ¼ cup jam and continue baking.
- **COMBINE** reserved juice, vinegar, honey, cornstarch, cinnamon and remaining ½ cup jam in medium saucepan. Heat to boiling. Reduce heat; cook and stir 2 minutes or until slightly thickened.
- **STIR** chopped pineapple into sauce; heat through. Serve warm over ham slices.

Nutrients per serving:

Calories 250
Total Fat 5g
Cholesterol 90mg
Sodium 1680mg
Carbohydrate 25g
Dietary Fiber 1g
Sugars 19g
Protein 28g

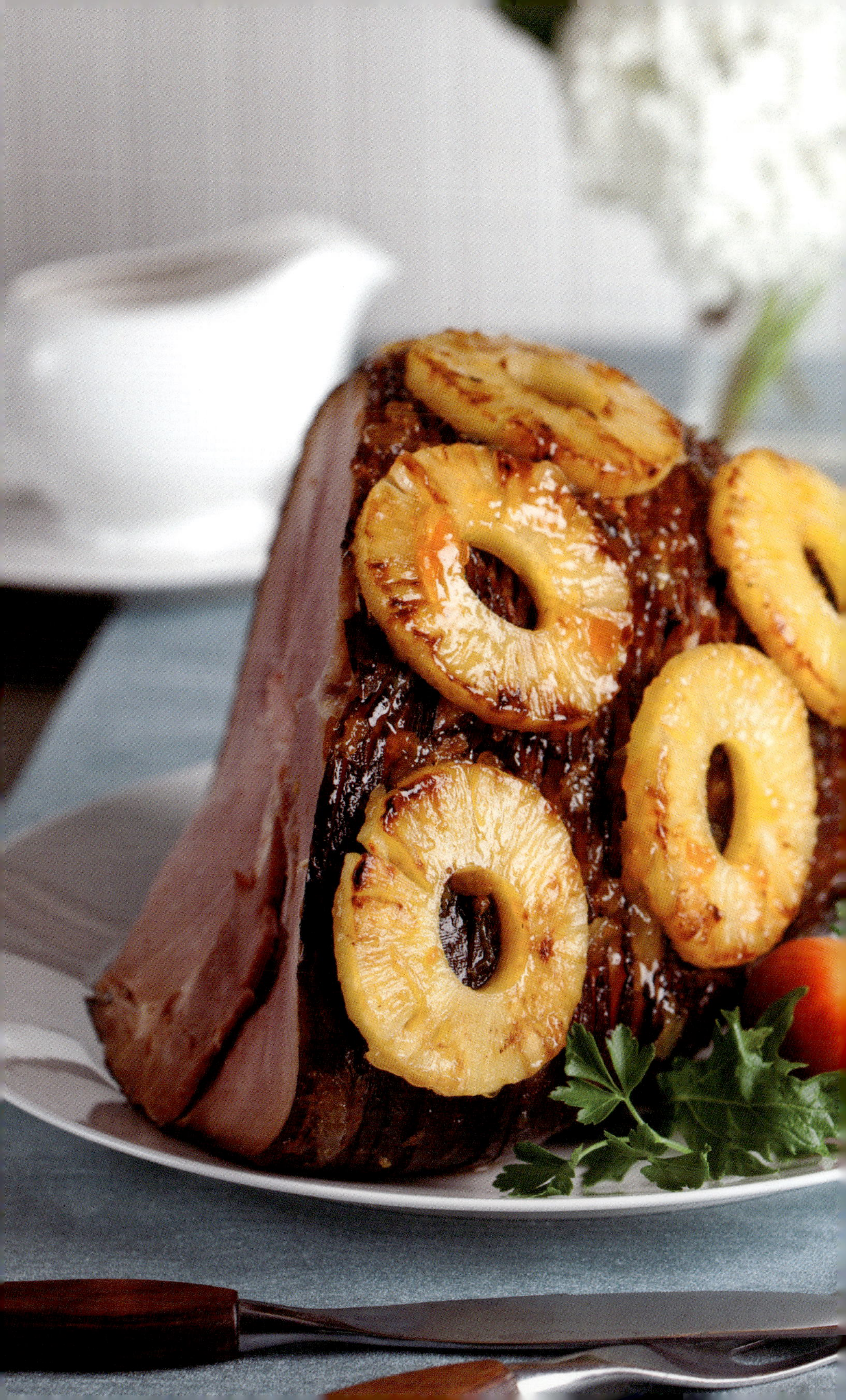

Citrus Barbecue Chicken

Prep: 10 min. • Grill: 20 min.
Makes 5 servings

- ½ cup barbecue sauce
- 1 teaspoon grated orange peel
- 1 teaspoon grated fresh ginger
- 5 boneless skinless chicken breasts
- 1 can (20 oz.) DOLE® Pineapple Slices

- **STIR** together barbecue sauce, orange peel and ginger in small bowl.
- **GRILL** or broil chicken breasts 8 minutes, brushing with half of sauce. Turn chicken over and add pineapple slices to grill. Brush chicken and pineapple with remaining sauce. Continue grilling 8 to 10 minutes or until chicken is no longer pink in center and slices are lightly browned. Garnish with chopped parsley, if desired.

Nutrients per serving:

Calories 220
Total Fat 3.5g
Cholesterol 75mg

Sodium 420mg
Carbohydrate 22g
Dietary Fiber 1g

Sugars 19g
Protein 28g

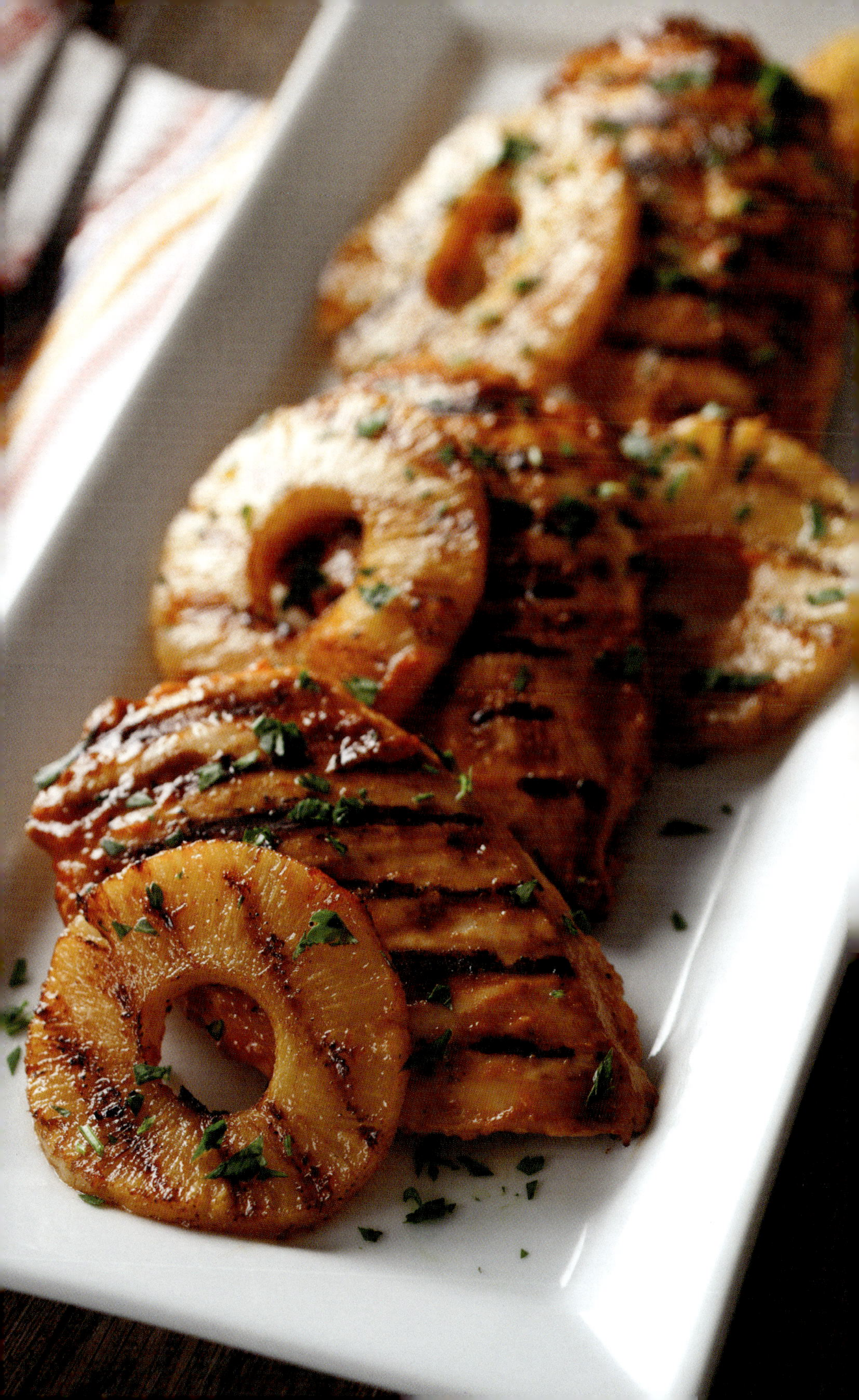

Polynesian Meatballs

Prep: 20 min. • Bake: 30 min.
Makes 5 to 6 servings

- 1 can (20 oz.) DOLE® Crushed Pineapple, divided
- 1 pkg. (20 oz.) ground turkey *or* chicken
- 2 cups instant brown rice, uncooked
- ¾ cup thinly sliced green onions, divided
- ½ cup teriyaki sauce, divided
- 1 egg, lightly beaten
- 1 teaspoon ground ginger
- ½ teaspoon ground nutmeg
- 2 tablespoons orange marmalade

- **PREHEAT** oven to 350°F. Drain ½ cup crushed pineapple for meatballs. Reserve remaining pineapple and juice for sauce. Line baking sheet with aluminum foil.

- **COMBINE** ground turkey, 2 cups rice, ½ cup drained pineapple, ½ cup green onions, ¼ cup teriyaki sauce, egg, ginger and nutmeg in large bowl, mixing well.

- **SCOOP** about ¼ cup turkey mixture and gently roll into desired meatball size; place on baking sheet. Repeat with remaining mixture. Bake 25 to 30 minutes.

- **MEANWHILE** to make sauce, combine remaining pineapple and juice, ¼ cup teriyaki sauce and orange marmalade in medium saucepan; heat to boiling. Reduce heat and simmer, uncovered, 3 to 4 minutes. Stir in remaining ¼ cup green onions.

- **TOP** meatballs with sauce. Serve over additional cooked rice and green onions, if desired.

Nutrients per serving:

Calories 320
Total Fat 3g
Cholesterol 65mg
Sodium 900mg
Carbohydrate 45g
Dietary Fiber 3g
Sugars 20g
Protein 29g

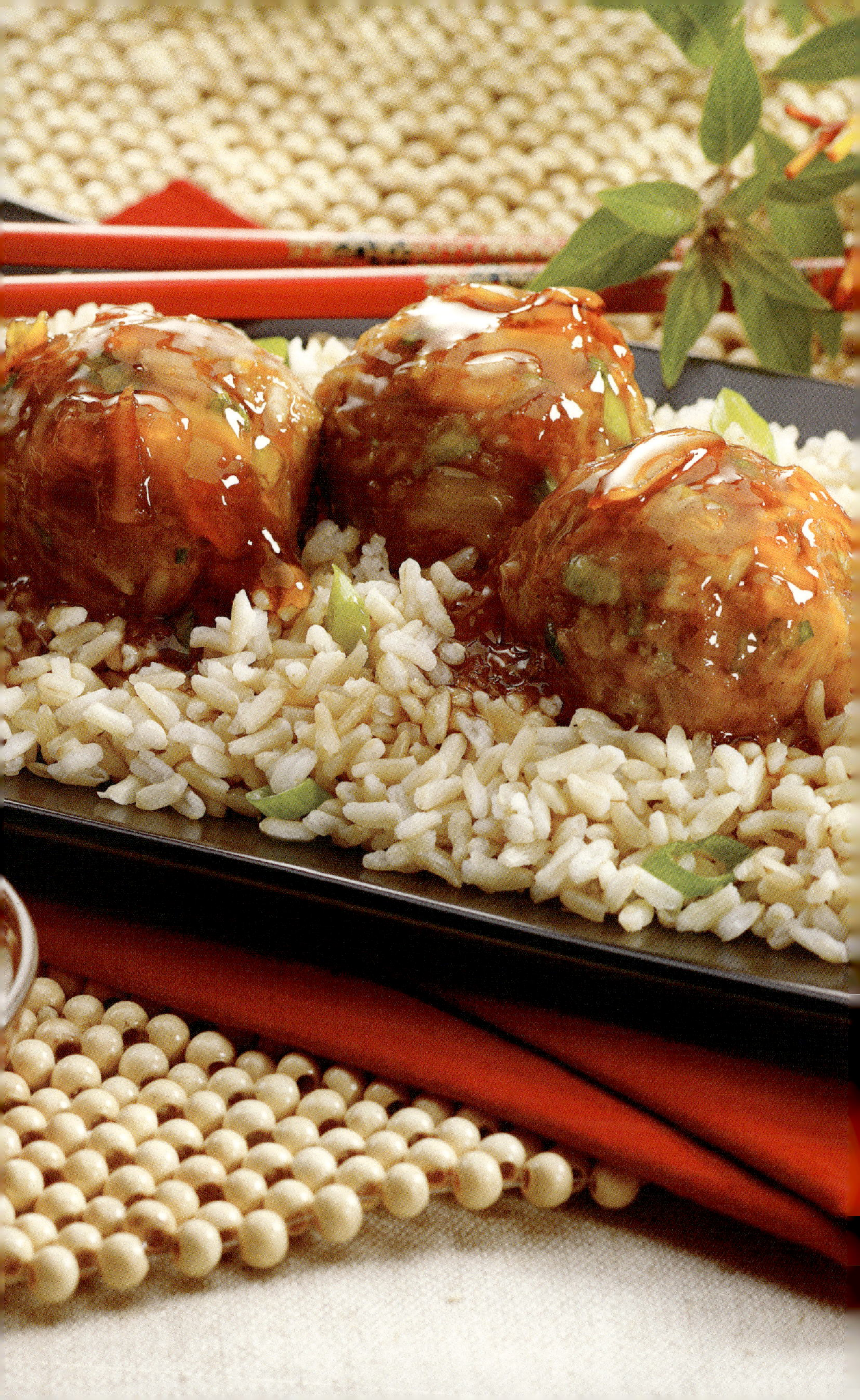

Bulgur Wheat with Pineapple, Pecans and Basil

Prep: 10 min. • Cook: 40 min.
Makes 4 servings

- 2 cups water
- 1 cup bulgur
- 1 can (20 oz.) DOLE® Pineapple Chunks, drained
- ½ cup chopped pecans
- 2 tablespoons chopped fresh basil
- 2 tablespoons chopped fresh Italian parsley
- 1½ teaspoons olive oil

- **COMBINE** water and bulgur in large saucepan. Heat to boiling, reduce heat and simmer, covered, 35 to 40 minutes or until bulgur is tender but not mushy.

- **TRANSFER** to large bowl; cool to room temperature.

- **STIR** pineapple chunks, pecans, basil, parsley and oil into bulgur. Serve at room temperature.

Nutrients per serving:

Calories 309
Total Fat 13g
Cholesterol 0mg

Sodium 21mg
Carbohydrate 46g
Dietary Fiber 9g

Sugars 16g
Protein 6g

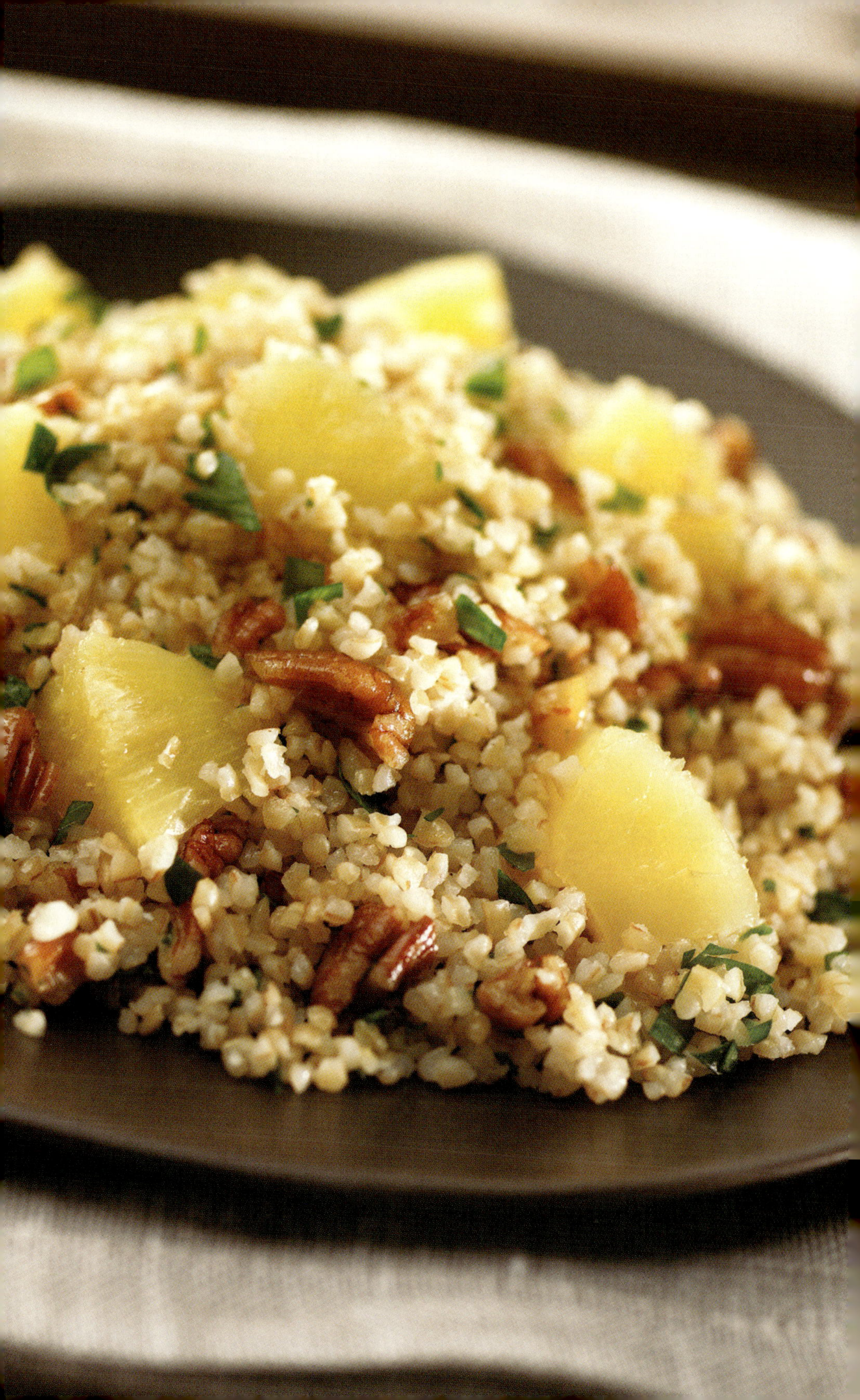

Carrot Date Slaw

**Prep: 25 min.
Makes 8 servings**

- 1 pkg. (14 oz.) DOLE® Classic Coleslaw
- 1 cup shredded DOLE Carrots
- 1 can (11 *or* 15 oz.) DOLE Mandarin Oranges, drained
- 12 DOLE Whole Pitted Dates, cut in thin strips
- ½ cup chopped hazelnuts, toasted
- Honey-Mustard Vinaigrette (recipe below)
- Salt and ground black pepper, to taste

- **COMBINE** coleslaw, carrots, mandarin oranges, dates and hazelnuts in bowl. Toss with Honey-Mustard Vinaigrette to evenly coat. Season with salt and black pepper, to taste.

Honey-Mustard Vinaigrette: Whisk together 3 tablespoons cider vinegar, 2 tablespoons Dijon mustard and 1 tablespoon honey in small bowl. Gradually whisk in 6 tablespoons olive oil, until dressing is thick and creamy. Makes about ¾ cup.

Nutrients per serving:

Calories 200
Total Fat 7g
Cholesterol 0mg

Sodium 45mg
Carbohydrate 34g
Dietary Fiber 5g

Sugars 31g
Protein 3g

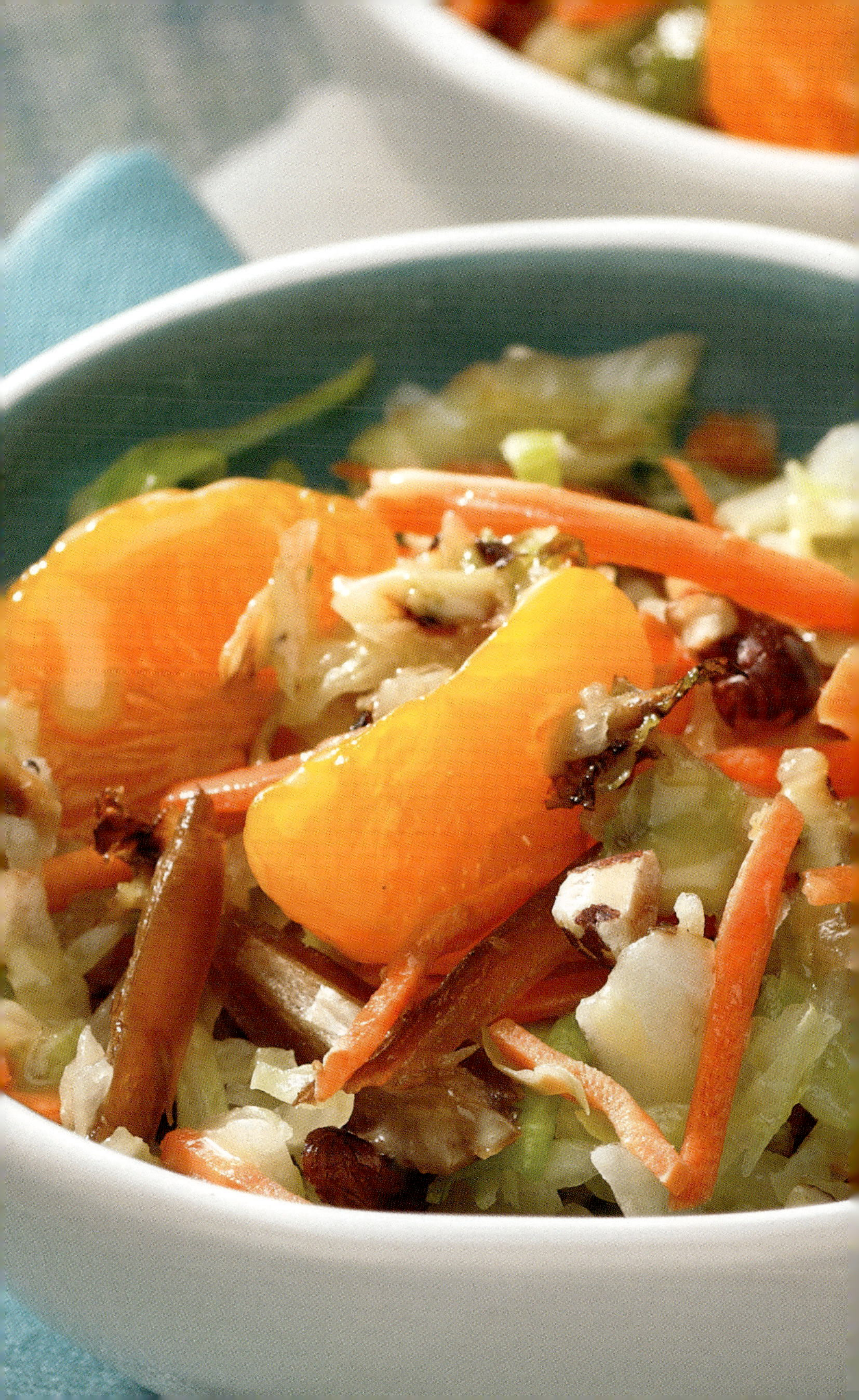

Watergate Salad

**Prep: 15 min. • Chill: 1 hr.
Makes 8 servings**

- 1 pkg. (4-serving size) pistachio instant pudding
- 1 can (20 oz.) DOLE® Crushed Pineapple, undrained
- 1 cup miniature marshmallows
- ½ cup chopped pecans
- 1½ cups (½ of 8-oz. tub) thawed whipped topping

- **MIX** dry pudding mix, pineapple, marshmallows and pecans in large bowl until well blended. Gently stir in whipped topping; cover.
- **REFRIGERATE** 1 hour or until ready to serve.

Nutrients per serving:

Calories 200	Sodium 190mg	Sugars 24g
Total Fat 7g	Carbohydrate 31g	Protein 1g
Cholesterol 0mg	Dietary Fiber 1g	

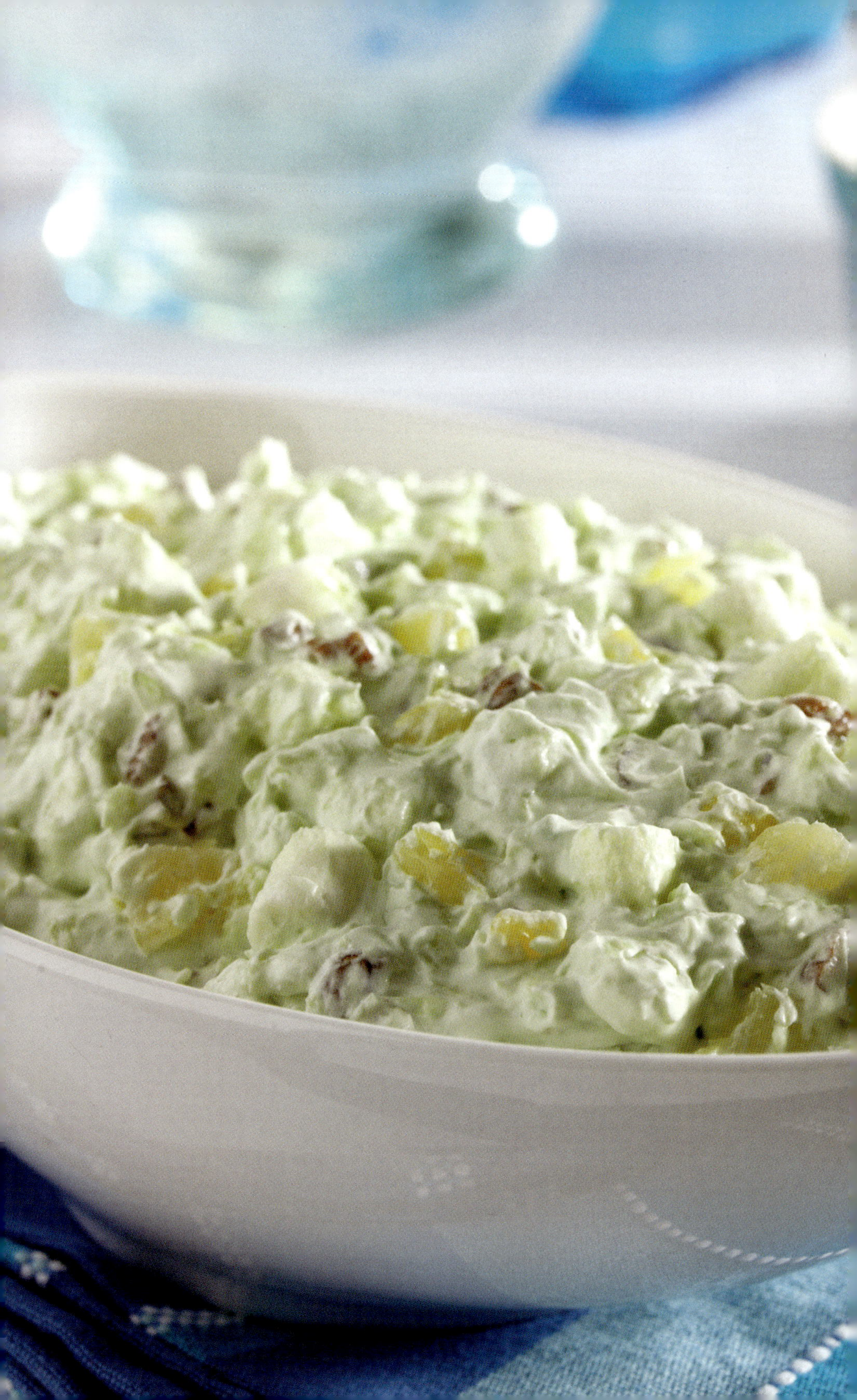

Easy Upside Down Cake

**Prep: 15 min. • Bake: 40 min.
Makes 10 servings**

1	can (20 oz.) DOLE® Pineapple Slices
¼	cup butter *or* margarine, melted
⅔	cup packed brown sugar
10	maraschino cherries
1	box (2 layer) yellow or pineapple-flavored cake mix

- **PREHEAT** oven to 350°F. Drain pineapple, reserving ¾ cup juice.

- **STIR** together melted butter and brown sugar in 12-inch skillet with heatproof handle. Arrange pineapple slices in sugar mixture. Place cherry in center of each pineapple slice.

- **PREPARE** cake mix according to package directions, replacing water with reserved ¾ cup juice. Pour batter evenly over pineapple.

- **BAKE** 40 to 45 minutes or until toothpick inserted in center comes out clean.

- **COOL** 5 minutes. Loosen edges and invert onto serving platter.

Note: Cake can be baked in 13×9-inch baking pan instead of skillet. Prepare and assemble cake as above except cut two pineapple slices in half and place whole slices along edges of pan and halved slices in center. Place cherries in center of slices. Bake and cool as above.

Mini Upside Down Cakes: Drain 1 can (20 oz.) DOLE Crushed Pineapple, reserving juice. Grease 24 muffin cups. Stir ⅓ cup melted butter with ⅔ cup packed brown sugar. Evenly spoon mixture into bottoms of cups; spoon about 1 tablespoon crushed pineapple over sugar mixture. Prepare cake mix as above. Evenly pour batter into cups. Bake 20 to 25 minutes. Invert onto serving platter. Makes 24 servings.

Nutrients per serving:

Calories 440	Sodium 380mg	Sugars 51g
Total Fat 19g	Carbohydrate 65g	Protein 5g
Cholesterol 70mg	Dietary Fiber 1g	

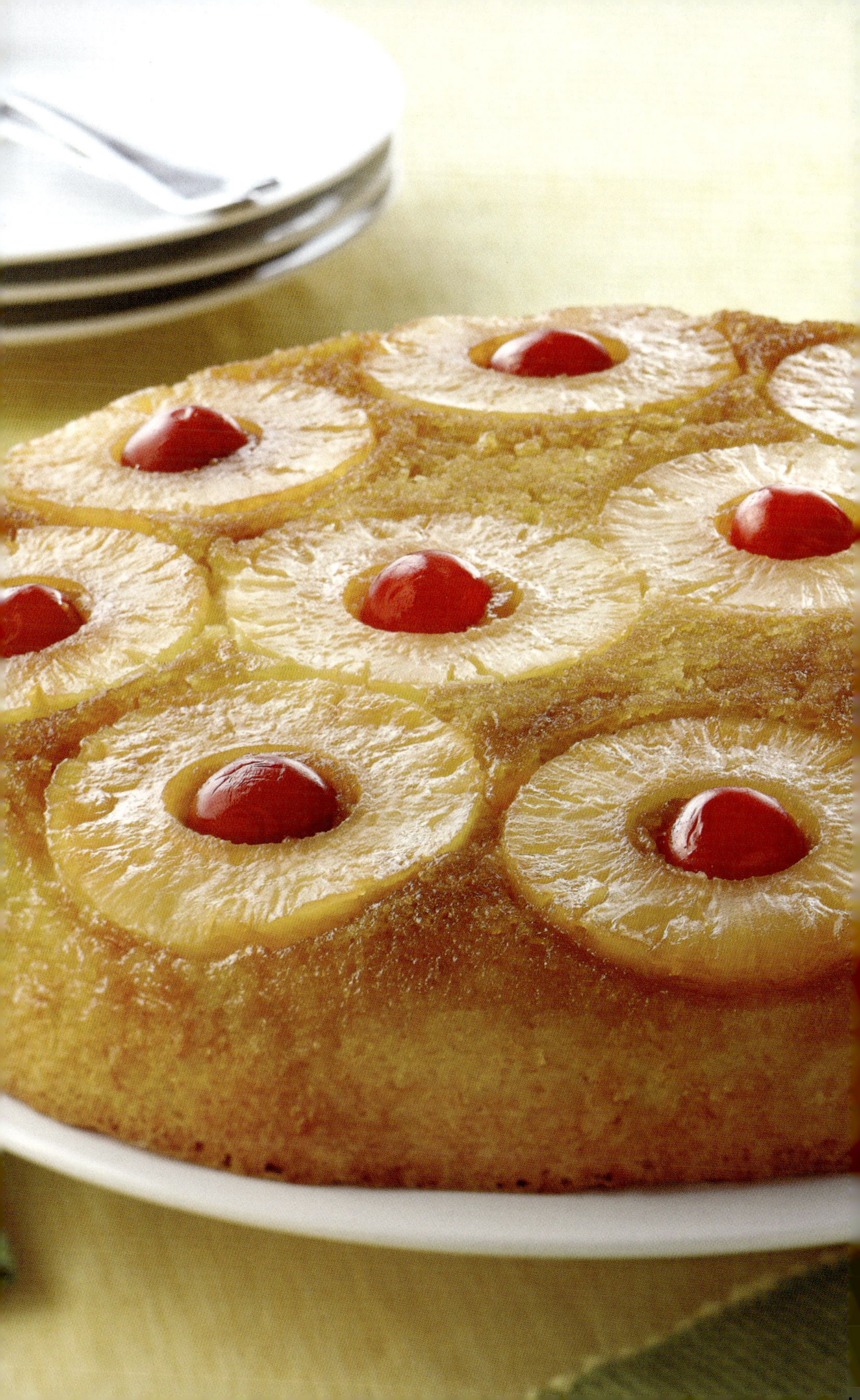

Easy Pineapple Rice Pudding

**Prep: 10 min.
Makes 10 to 12 servings**

- 4 cups cold milk
- 2 pkgs. (4-serving size each) instant vanilla pudding
- 4 cups cooked white rice, cooled
- 1 can (20 oz.) DOLE® Pineapple Chunks, drained
- ½ cup DOLE Seedless Raisins
- 1 teaspoon ground cinnamon
- 1 teaspoon vanilla extract

- **WHISK** together milk and pudding mix in large bowl, 2 to 3 minutes.
- **STIR** in rice, pineapple chunks, raisins, cinnamon and vanilla. Refrigerate until ready to serve.

Nutrients per serving:

Calories 230
Total Fat 1g
Cholesterol 5mg

Sodium 300mg
Carbohydrate 48g
Dietary Fiber 1g

Sugars 28g
Protein 5g

30